MW00532955

Designer - Chris Treccani www.3dogcreative.net
Illustrator - Alice Calder
Editor - Katherine Rawson

Blog
www.cocktailhourmeets.com

Instagram
CocktailHourMeets

Facebook Group
Cocktail Hour Meets

ISBN 978-0-578-79171-5   Paperback
ISBN 978-0-578-79172-2   ePub

Cocktail Hour Meets...
A PRESIDENTIAL ELECTION

Surviving a Presidential election
amidst a pandemic.

Because even when you
don't know what day it is,
there's still cocktail hour!

Jeremy Cooper
Andy Klausner

Table of Contents

Foreword   7

Day 1 - Whiskey Rebellion - George Washington   10
Day 2 - Quiveration - John Adams   12
Day 3 - The Architect - Thomas Jefferson   14
Day 4 - Bumbo - James Madison   16
Day 5 - The Last Cocked Hat - James Monroe   18
Day 6 - Skinny Dipper - John Quincy Adams   20
Day 7 - The Cursing Parrot - Andrew Jackson   22
Day 8 - The Old Kinderhook - Martin Van Buren   24
Day 9 - Old Tippecanoe - William Henry Harrison   26
Day 10 - Quince Hijos - John Tyler   28
Day 11 - Party Pooper - James K. Polk   30
Day 12 - The Deadly Cherry - Zachary Taylor   32
Day 13 - Uninspired - Millard Fillmore   34
Day 14 - The Bender - Franklin Pierce   36
Day 15 - The Bachelor - James Buchanan   38
Day 16 - An Unfortunate Night at the Theater - Abraham Lincoln   40
Day 17 - The Tennessee Tailor - Andrew Johnson   42
Day 18 - "S" Stands For ... Sangre - Ulysses S. Grant   44
Day 19 - Rutherfraud - Rutherford B. Hayes   46
Day 20 - Athenian Romano - James Garfield   48
Day 21 - Elegant Arthur - Chester A. Arthur   50
Day 22 - 21 & Done - Grover Cleveland   52
Day 23 - Human Iceberg - Benjamin Harrison   54
Day 24 - Grover: Take 2 - Grover Cleveland   56
Day 25 - The Carnation - William McKinley   58
Day 26 - The Unlucky Valentine - Theodore Roosevelt   60
Day 27 - Billy Possum - William Howard Taft   62

Day 28 - The 25th Amendment - Woodrow Wilson   64
Day 29 - The Wandering Eye - Warren G. Harding   66
Day 30 - Vaseline - Calvin Coolidge   68
Day 31 - The Mandarin - Herbert Hoover   70
Day 32 - Private Fala - Franklin D. Roosevelt   72
Day 33 - The Buck Stops Here - Harry S. Truman   74
Day 34 - Camp Shangri-la - Dwight D. Eisenhower   76
Day 35 - The Boy Scout - John F. Kennedy   78
Day 36 - Wabash Cannonball - Lyndon B. Johnson   80
Day 37 - Deep Throat - Richard M. Nixon   82
Day 38 - Accidental President - Gerald R. Ford   84
Day 39 - Playboy Surprise - Jimmy Carter   86
Day 40 - Bedtime for Bonzo - Ronald Reagan   88
Day 41 - Bushusuru - George H. W. Bush   90
Day 42 - The Leftie - Bill Clinton   92
Day 43 - The Marathon Man - George W. Bush   94
Day 44 - O'Bomber - Barack Obama   96
Day 45 - You're Fired - Donald J. Trump   98
Day 46 - #NoMalarkey - Joe Biden   100

Epilogue   103
About the Authors   105

For consideration in any pandemic: Feel free to use any variation of the spirit or mixer that you have on hand.

Foreword

When our world was turned upside down in mid-March, we had no idea the magnitude of the pandemic or how long it would last (and as we write this book, we still do not). Ironically, we were initially concerned that our first book *Cocktail Hour Meets . . . A Pandemic* would be outdated by the time it was published in July 2020. Now, we consider it volume 1 of ongoing uncertainty and disruption.

Amidst the continuing pandemic, which to-date has taken more than 200,000 American lives and precipitated global economic devastation, 2020 continued with, arguably, the most important election of our lifetimes. The concept for this volume of *Cocktail Hour Meets* arose during one of our daily pandemic walks. The goal was to produce another fun and light-hearted cocktail-driven chronicle, providing some liquid inspiration before and after the confetti fell, and to learn along the way a little more about the qualities and idiosyncrasies of our presidents and their times. As noted in *A Pandemic*, we do not—by any stretch of the imagination—claim to be mixologists or professional photographers; similarly, for this volume, we also do not claim to be biographers or historians!

So, we did this: 45 cocktails in 45 days, starting on September 20, 2020, and ending on election day, November 3, 2020. A cocktail named in honor (memory, respect, or lampoon) of each of the 45 presidents of the United States. We added a 46th cocktail in honor of president-elect Biden* We posted a picture of each cocktail on Instagram (CocktailHourMeets) and Facebook (Cocktail Hour Meets) each night with a brief explanation of the naming. Immediately following the election, we wrote the Epilogue with our personal reflections on the ups and downs of our lead-up-to-the-election experience and on our hopes for the future of our great nation.

One key point and guiding principle of the book: it is meant to be non-partisan (not to say there isn't some occasional good-spirited needling—all in the true spirit of cocktail hour itself). Our only political agenda here is to advocate for the right for all those eligible to be able to vote safely, securely, and conveniently. Thus our commitment to donate a portion of sales from this book to Vote.org (www.vote.org).

So, how to make this fun and informative . . . dare we venture educational? Each cocktail is accompanied by five interesting tidbits about each president that most probably don't know (we sure didn't). And then, because Jeremy is a little geeky that way, we've given a timeline of significant events that occurred during each president's tenure to provide historical context.

We don't say five events like we do tidbits because, Google as we may, we couldn't find five significant events that happened under each president. Our past presidents are a diverse group, kind of like our days living through this pandemic—some memorable, some wholly forgettable. It's also hard to expect a lot to happen when a guy is only in office for 33 days (William Henry Harrison). On the flip side, some of these men presided during so many consequential events that we could have had many more than five bullets. In those cases, we may have taken liberties with the "bullets" to cram the important stuff in. For the sake of space, we did not give long explanations of each historical event. If something peaks your curiosity or tickles your fancy, please GTS! And if you discover any errors in our "facts," they were made unintentionally, and we blame the World Wide Web (where we sometimes found conflicting information).

As to the cocktails themselves, we did some research into the drinking (and eating) habits of each president and when possible included ingredients (both alcoholic and nonalcoholic) that seemed relevant. As with everything else in our research, coming up with ingredients for some cocktails was easy (hint: George Washington) and others more difficult (Abraham Lincoln, whose favorite drink was water)! You might have to do some research of your own if you are interested in discovering the historical relevance of some of the ingredients we chose. Since this is a cocktail book, we decided to use cocktails instead of mocktails even for the teetotaling presidents.

So, pleasing cocktails, a chance to get your Jeopardese on, and some comradery along the way: we are all in this together.

We hope that you enjoy the book and please test and improve upon a cocktail or two or three along the way!

*While Biden has been declared president-elect as we go to publication, the Trump campaign is actively seeking recounts and both campaigns are filing lawsuits. While we do not feel that the election outcome will change – experts report #nomalarkey in the voting –we note the possibility for completeness. In such an event, you get a bonus cocktail!

George Washington (1789 – 1797)

- After he instituted a tax on distilled spirits, tax collectors were the target of threats and violence. He subsequently led troops to quell what became known as the Whiskey Rebellion.
- He ran a distillery at Mount Vernon after his retirement that became one of the largest whiskey producers in the country.
- He and James Madison were the only two presidents who signed the Declaration of Independence.
- His dentures were not made of wood—they were actually made of hippopotamus ivory, bone, animal and human teeth, lead, brass screws, and gold wire. Some historians believe that his fondness for red wine might have stained them, making them look like wood.
- He only had a grade-school education.

INGREDIENTS

1 ½ ounces Rowan's Creek Kentucky bourbon whiskey
½ ounce Campari
½ ounce Luxardo cherry liqueur
½ ounce pure cherry juice
Garnish: Luxardo maraschino cherry

PREPARATION

Combine all ingredients in a cocktail shaker with ice and shake well. Strain into an ice-filled rocks glass. Garnish with cherry.

1789	1791	1792	1793	1794	
The French Revolution broke out with the storming of the Bastille prison		The U.S. Postal Service was established		The Slave Trade Act limited American involvement in the international trade of slaves	
	The Bill of Rights, which details specific rights and protections of Americans relative to the federal government, was ratified		Eli Whitney invented the cotton gin, hastening the Industrial Revolution		

It is far better to be alone, than to be in bad company.
–George Washington

John Adams (1797 – 1801)

- He suffered from a hand tremor he nicknamed "Quiveration."
- He was the first president to live in the White House.
- He wanted presidents to be addressed as "His Highness," which led some opponents to nickname him "His Rotundity."
- He is one of three presidents to die on July 4th (the others were Jefferson and Monroe).
- He was the only non-Virginian among the first five presidents.

INGREDIENTS

1 ounce Roger Grouth Pays d'Auge Calvados
1 ½ ounces Mount Gay Black Barrel Double Cask Blend rum
½ ounce lime juice
Henry Hotspur's Hard Pressed cider
Garnish: orange wheel

PREPARATION

Combine Calvados, rum and lime juice in a cocktail shaker with ice and shake-shake-shake well. Strain into an ice-filled highball glass. Top off with cider. Garnish with orange wheel.

1797	1797	1798	1800	1800	

The XYZ Affair brought the U.S. and France to the brink of war, resulting in the first military build-up of our new nation — **1797**

Pope Pius VI was taken prisoner by Napoleon Bonaparte and transported to France, where he died one year later — **1798**

Washington D.C., carved from Virginia and Maryland, became the capital of the nation and a federal zone — **1800**

1797 — The U.S.S. *Constitution*, "Old Ironsides," was launched and remained in commission through the 21st century

1800 — The Library of Congress was established

*Old minds are like old horses; you must exercise them
if you wish to keep them in working order.*
–John Adams

Thomas Jefferson (1801 – 1809)

- He was an architect and designed the rotundas at the University of Virginia and the Virginia State Capitol.
- It took him almost 40 years to build Monticello, which he also designed.
- He was a wine aficionado (Monticello had a wine cellar and two vineyards).
- He was an amateur archaeologist who collected fossils, including a complete mastodon.
- He hated public speaking so much that he only gave two speeches during his presidency—one each term. His State of the Union addresses were presented to Congress as written documents.

INGREDIENTS

1 ounce Espolón tequila reposado
¾ ounce D'Oliveiras "Meio Doce" 5-Year Madeira
¾ ounce Don Benigno amantillado sherry
½ ounce Luxardo apricot liqueur
Fever-Tree sparkling lemon
Garnish: lemon wedge

PREPARATION

Combine tequila, madiera, sherry and apricot liqueur in a cocktail shaker with ice and shake well. Strain into an ice-filled highball glass. Top off with sparkling lemon. Garnish with lemon wedge.

1801	1803	1804	1805	1808
The U.S. (aboard the U.S.S. *Constitution*) joined Sweden in the First Barbary War, fighting pirates from North Africa		The exploration of the Northwest by Lewis and Clark commenced		Ludwig von Beethoven composed his Symphony No. 5
	The Louisiana Purchase added 828,000 square miles of new territory to the U.S. for about $350 million in today's dollars		Upon her husband's death, Madame Clicquot Ponsardin took over the business in Champagne	

*Whenever you do a thing, act as if
all the world were watching.*
–Thomas Jefferson

James Madison (1809 – 1817)

- He felt that he lost an election for the Virginia House of Delegates because he refused to give voters alcohol on Election Day (a common practice referred to as "swilling the planters with bumbo.")
- He was introduced by Aaron Burr to his very popular wife, Dolly, who was 17 years younger.
- He was the smallest president at 5'4" and weighed around 100 pounds.
- Both of his vice presidents died in office during his terms.
- He appeared on a U.S. currency—the $5,000 bill, which was in circulation until President Nixon ordered it recalled in 1969.

INGREDIENTS

1 ounce Vieux Marc de Champagne
Kirkland Champagne brut
Garnish: Luxardo maraschino
    cherry

PREPARATION

Pour Marc de Champagne into champagne flute. Top off with Champagne. Garnish with cherry.

1811 — Construction of the Cumberland Road commenced in Maryland, connecting the Potomac and Ohio Rivers

1812 — The War of 1812 between the U.S. and Great Britain began

1814 — The British burned the city of Washington D.C. to the ground

1814 — Francis Scott Key wrote "The Star-Spangled Banner"; Congress declared it the national anthem 117 years later

1815 — Napoleon was defeated at Waterloo

Philosophy is common sense with big words.
–James Madison

James Monroe (1817 – 1825)

- He had a penchant for wearing outdated Revolutionary War era clothes, inspiring his nickname "The Last Cocked Hat."
- He ran unopposed for reelection—the only other president to do so was George Washington.
- He is the soldier holding the flag in the famous painting *Washington Crossing the Delaware* by Emanuel Leutze.
- He was a law apprentice for Thomas Jefferson.
- He was the last surviving "Founding Father."

INGREDIENTS

3 ounces Diplomático Reserva Exclusiva rum
1 ounce San Gregoria Old Vines Garnacha
½ ounce agave syrup
Topo Chico

PREPARATION

Combine rum, wine and agave syrup in a cocktail shaker with ice and shake well. Strain into a wine glass. Top off with Topo Chico.

The 49th parallel was set as the border with Canada

The Panic of 1819, in the aftermath of the Napoleonic Wars, was the first widespread financial crisis in the U.S.

The Monroe Doctrine was delivered to Congress, shaping U.S. policy in the Western Hemisphere going forward

1818   1818   1819   1820   1823

Congress deemed the number of stripes on the U.S. flag to be 13 to honor the original colonies

The Missouri Compromise established a balance of power between free and slave states

*National honor is the national property
of the highest value.*
–James Monroe

John Quincy Adams (1825 – 1829)

- He was known to skinny dip in the Potomac River every morning.
- He was involved in a four-way presidential race in which no candidates received the necessary electoral votes. He won in a runoff vote, held by the House, in spite of having finished last in the electoral college and losing the popular vote.
- He is considered one of the greatest diplomats of all time and the driving force behind the Monroe Doctrine.
- He argued a case before the Supreme Court (and won), having previously declined a nomination to the high court from President Monroe.
- He became a lawyer without going to law school.

INGREDIENTS

3 ounces Blandy's 5-year bual Madiera
1 ½ ounces De Luze VS cognac
½ ounce Liber & Co. Fiery ginger syrup
1 ounce pineapple juice
Pinch of ground nutmeg
Garnish: rosemary sprig

PREPARATION

Combine madiera, cognac, ginger syrup and pineapple juice in a cocktail shaker with ice and shake well. Strain into an ice-filled high-ball glass. Sprinkle nutmeg on top. Garnish with rosemary sprig.

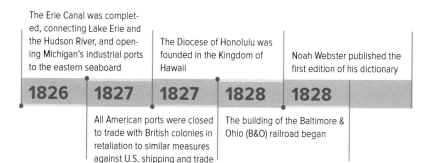

The Erie Canal was completed, connecting Lake Erie and the Hudson River, and opening Michigan's industrial ports to the eastern seaboard

The Diocese of Honolulu was founded in the Kingdom of Hawaii

Noah Webster published the first edition of his dictionary

1826 **1827** **1827** **1828** **1828**

All American ports were closed to trade with British colonies in retaliation to similar measures against U.S. shipping and trade

The building of the Baltimore & Ohio (B&O) railroad began

Courage and perserverance have a magical effect, before which difficulties disappear and obstacles vanish into air.

–John Quincy Adams

Andrew Jackson (1829 – 1837)

- He was rumored to have taught his parrot to curse. The parrot allegedly had to be removed from his funeral because it would not stop cussing.
- He was involved in many duels, killing a man who had called him a "worthless scoundrel, a poltroon, and a coward."
- He is the only president to have been a prisoner of war (Revolutionary War).
- The national debt was paid off during his presidency—the first and only time in U.S. history.
- He appears on the $20 bill even though he was opposed to paper money.

INGREDIENTS

1 ½ ounces Bushmills Irish whiskey
½ ounce Disaronno amaretto
½ ounce Twisted Alchemy
    blood orange juice

PREPARATION

Combine all ingredients in a cocktail shaker with ice and shake well. Strain into an ice-filled rocks glass.

1829	1830	1830	1831	1836
James Smithson bequeathed his estate to found the Smithsonian Institution		Greece was liberated from the Ottoman Empire and granted citizenship to its Jewish residents		The Battle of the Alamo was fought in the Texas Revolution
	The Underground Railroad was established		Leopold I became the first king of Belgium following its recognition by the Great Powers the prior year	

Take time to deliberate; but when the time for action arrives, stop thinking and go in.
–Andrew Jackson

Martin Van Buren (1837 – 1841)

- He was nicknamed "Little Magician" because he was only 5'6" tall, and "Sly Fox" because of his political prowess. The word "Okay" or "OK" originated with his other nickname "Old Kinder-hook," which was his birthplace in N.Y. state.
- He is the first president to be born as a citizen of the U.S.
- He is the only president to-date to speak English as a second language. His first language was Dutch, having been born in a town of Dutch settlers.
- Because his wife had died, his daughter-in-law assumed First Lady duties.
- After the stock market crashed in 1837, he got yet another new nickname— Martin Van Ruin.

INGREDIENTS

2 ounces Johnnie Walker Swing blended scotch whisky
1 ounce De Luze VS cognac
½ tablespoon Trader Joe's fig butter
Fever-Tree Elderflower tonic water

PREPARATION

Combine scotch whisky, cognac and fig butter in a cocktail shaker with ice and shake well. Strain into an ice-filled rocks glass. Top off with tonic water.

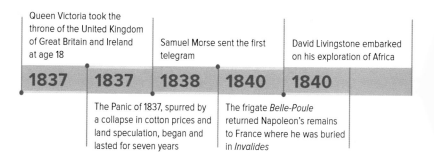

Queen Victoria took the throne of the United Kingdom of Great Britain and Ireland at age 18

Samuel Morse sent the first telegram

David Livingstone embarked on his exploration of Africa

1837 **1837** **1838** **1840** **1840**

The Panic of 1837, spurred by a collapse in cotton prices and land speculation, began and lasted for seven years

The frigate *Belle-Poule* returned Napoleon's remains to France where he was buried in *Invalides*

*It is easier to do a job right than
to explain why you didn't.*
–Martin Van Buren

William Henry Harrison (1841 – 1841)

- He was nicknamed "Old Tippecanoe" for his victory at the Battle of Tippecanoe.
- He gave the longest inauguration speech on record (8,445 words and over 90 minutes).
- He was the first president to die in office after falling ill soon after his inauguration speech (given on a cold, wet day). He had the shortest tenure of any president in history as well—33 days.
- He actually wanted to be a doctor, but had to drop out of medical school because he could not afford the tuition.
- Six of his ten children died before he became president, but his son Benjamin became the 23rd president of the U.S.

INGREDIENTS

1 ounce Absolut Elyx vodka
4 ounces Henry Hotspur's hard pressed cider
3 ½ ounces Fever-Tree ginger beer
½ ounce lime juice
Pinch of ground allspice
Garnish: lime wheel

PREPARATION

Combine vodka, cider, ginger beer and lime juice in an ice-filled copper mule mug. Sprinkle allspice on top. Garnish with lime wheel.

Harrison was not president long enough for much of anything to happen!

1841

Times change, and we change with them.
–William Henry Harrison

John Tyler (1841 – 1845)

- He had 15 children, the most of any president in history.
- After Harrison's death, there was some question whether as vice president he should become president—but he did and the line of succession became official.
- He was very unpopular and was expelled from his party during his presidency. He was also the first president to face impeachment.
- He was the first president to have a veto overriden by Congress.
- The city of Tyler, Texas, was named after him because he convinced the Senate to annex Texas.

INGREDIENTS

2 ounces Tanteo Habañero tequila

4 scoops mango sorbet

1 ounce Twisted Alchemy Persian lime sour juice

Kirkland Champagne brut

PREPARATION

Purée sorbet, tequila and Persian lime sour juice in blender until smooth. Pour into four shot glasses. Top off with Champagne.

1842	1842	1842	1844	1845	

Labor unions were legalized in the U.S. (1842)

The first Opium War between Britain and China ended with the Treaty of Nanking and the ceding of governance of Hong Kong until 1997 (1842)

The Texas Annexation Treaty was signed on Tyler's last day in office (1845)

The first settlers reached the Oregon Territory (1842)

The Treaty of Wanghia was signed with the Qing dynasty, marking the U.S.'s first diplomatic agreement with China (1844)

Wealth can only be accumulated by the earnings of industry and the savings of frugality.
—John Tyler

James K. Polk (1845 – 1849)

- He banned booze, card playing, and dancing in the White House.
- He was a compromise "dark horse" candidate who nobody expected to win, but received the nomination when delegates at the Democratic convention were deadlocked.
- He held "office hours" two days every week where any citizen could drop in just to talk or to lobby for a cause.
- He oversaw the greatest territorial expansion of any president and campaigned with the slogan "54-40 or fight," referring to the latitude line he believed should be the nation's northern border in Oregon.
- He was instrumental in the construction of the Washington Monument.

INGREDIENTS

2 ½ ounces Don Benigno amantillado sherry
1 ounce Tanteo Jalapeño tequila
¼ ounce Liber & Co. Fiery ginger syrup
½ ounce lime juice
1 ounce Mr Q. Cumber sparkling cucumber beverage
Garnish: two cucumber slices

PREPARATION

Combine sherry, tequila, ginger syrup and lime juice in a cocktail shaker with ice and shake well. Strain into an ice-filled highball glass. Top off with sparkling cucumber beverage. Garnish with cucumber slices.

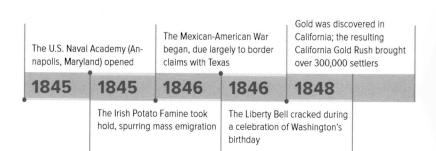

1845	1845	1846	1846	1848
	The U.S. Naval Academy (Annapolis, Maryland) opened	The Mexican-American War began, due largely to border claims with Texas		Gold was discovered in California; the resulting California Gold Rush brought over 300,000 settlers
		The Irish Potato Famine took hold, spurring mass emigration	The Liberty Bell cracked during a celebration of Washington's birthday	

No president who performs his duties faithfully and conscientiously can have any leisure.
–James K. Polk

Zachary Taylor (1849 – 1850)

- He is believed to have died from gastroenteritis soon after eating a snack of highly acidic cherries with fresh milk while attending a Fourth of July celebration.
- He was a descendent of William Brewster, a leader of the Pilgrims who sailed on the *Mayflower* and landed at Plymouth Rock.
- His nickname was "Old Rough-and-Ready"—rough from his clothing and ready because he was always ready to fight.
- His daughter Sarah was married for three months to Jefferson Davis (future president of the Confederacy) before succumbing to malaria.
- He was nominated to be president by the Whig Party without his knowledge and was notified by mail that he was their candidate.

INGREDIENTS

1 ½ ounces Woodford Reserve bourbon whiskey
½ ounce lemon juice
1 teaspoon Luxardo maraschino cherry syrup
S. Pellegrino Essenza Cherry & Pomegranate sparkling water
Garnish: Luxardo maraschino cherry and lemon twist

PREPARATION

Combine whiskey, lemon juice and cherry syrup in a cocktail shaker with ice and shake well. Strain into an ice-filled highball glass. Top off with sparkling water. Garnish with cherry and lemon twist.

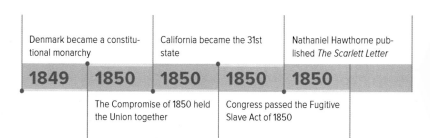

Denmark became a constitutional monarchy	California became the 31st state		Nathaniel Hawthorne published *The Scarlett Letter*
1849	**1850**	**1850**	**1850**	**1850**
	The Compromise of 1850 held the Union together	Congress passed the Fugitive Slave Act of 1850	

*I have always done my duty. I am ready to die.
My only regret is for the friends I leave behind me.*
–Zachary Taylor

Millard Fillmore (1850 – 1853)

- The official White House website calls him "uninspiring," and he is considered by many to be one of the worst presidents in history.
- He did not have a vice president. The Constitution did not have a provision about the office, which has been vacant for 38 years of the nation's history.
- He established the White House Library.
- When he heard that the Library of Congress was on fire, he ran there to help put the fire out.
- He married his teacher Abigail Powers.

INGREDIENTS

3 ounces Blandy's 5-year bual Madiera
1 ounce Aniché XO Double Wood rum
Fever-Tree sparkling pink grapefruit
Fee Brothers grapefruit bitters (2 dashes)
Garnish: Tillen Farms Rum Bada Bing cherry

PREPARATION

Combine Madiera, rum and bitters in an ice-filled wine glass. Add bitters. Top off with sparkling pink grapefruit. Garnish with cherry.

1850	1851	1851	1852	1852
Gold was found in the Oregon Territory		Rama IV, on whom the musical *The King and I* is based, was crowned King of Siam		*Uncle Tom's Cabin*, written by Harriet Beecher Stowe, was published
	The Great Exhibition was held at the Crystal Palace in London, becoming the first World Fair		Commodore Matthew Perry began his mission to Japan	

*Let us remember that revolutions do not always
establish freedom.*
–Millard Filmore

Franklin Pierce (1853 – 1857)

- He was known to be an alcoholic and died from cirrhosis of the liver.
- He was so unpopular while in office that his own party did not renominate him for a second term.
- He is the only president not to use a Bible at his inauguration. He used a law book instead.
- He was the first president to have a Christmas tree in the White House.
- He had three sons, all of whom died in childhood.

INGREDIENTS

1 ½ ounces Havana Club Selección Maestros 90-proof Cuban rum

½ ounce Diamond Reserve 151-proof Demara rum

1 ounce Twisted Alchemy blood orange juice

½ ounce Twisted Alchemy Persian lime juice

1 teaspoon Tillen Farms Rum Bada Bing cherry juice

Garnish: Tillen Farms Rum Bada Bing cherry

PREPARATION

Combine all ingredients in a cocktail shaker with ice and shake well. Strain into an ice-filled highball glass. Garnish with cherry.

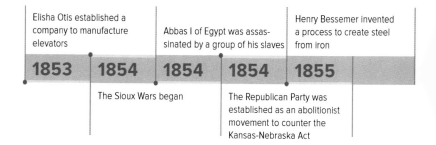

1853	1854	1854	1854	1855
Elisha Otis established a company to manufacture elevators		Abbas I of Egypt was assassinated by a group of his slaves		Henry Bessemer invented a process to create steel from iron
	The Sioux Wars began		The Republican Party was established as an abolitionist movement to counter the Kansas-Nebraska Act	

You have summoned me in my weakness.
You must sustain me in your strength.
–Franklin Pierce

James Buchanan (1857 – 1861)

- He was the only bachelor to be president.
- He was rumored to be gay because of his close relationship with Alabama Senator William Rufus King (they lived together for 10 years).
- He was often called "doughface," which meant that he was a northerner who favored southern opinions.
- He had two different colored eyes—one green and one brown.
- He raised pygmy goats in the White House Rose Garden.

INGREDIENTS

1 ounce Don Benigno amantillado sherry
1 ounce "1" tequila blanco
¾ ounce Cointreau orange liqueu
½ ounce lime juice
½ ounce pineapple juice
Garnish: orange wheel

PREPARATION

Combine all ingredients in a cockt
shaker with ice and shake well.
Strain into an ice-filled highball
glass. Garnish with orange wheel.

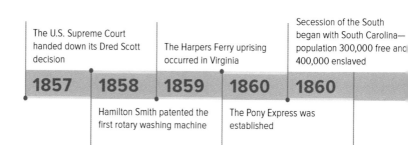

1857	1858	1859	1860	1860
The U.S. Supreme Court handed down its Dred Scott decision		The Harpers Ferry uprising occurred in Virginia		Secession of the South began with South Carolina—population 300,000 free and 400,000 enslaved
	Hamilton Smith patented the first rotary washing machine		The Pony Express was established	

What is right and what is practicable are two different things.
–James Buchanan

Abraham Lincoln (1861 – 1865)

- A bill to create the secret service was on his desk the night of his assassination.
- A stovepipe top hat was more than his signature look – he stored important documents in it.
- He was often called the president of firsts—he was the first president to hold a patent, the first to have an inauguration photo, and the first to have a full beard.
- He was the tallest president at 6'4".
- He had lost five previous elections (for various offices) before he was elected president.

INGREDIENTS

1 ½ ounces Tanteo Cocoa tequila
½ ounce Amarula cream liqueur
Topo Chico
Garnish: Hershey's mint cookie
     layer crunch

PREPARATION

Blend tequila, cream liqueur and ice in blender until smooth. Pour into martini glass. Top off with Topo Chico. Place cookie on rim of glass.

1861	1862	1863	1865	1865
The Confederate States of America was created		Lincoln issued the Emancipation Proclamation, the Battle of Gettysburg was fought, and the Gettysburg Address was given		The Confederate army surrendered at Appomattox
	Otto von Bismarck became prime minister of Prussia and presented his vision for unification of Germany		Slavery was abolished by the 13th Amendment to the Constitution	

*No man has a good enough memory
to be a successful liar.*
–Abraham Lincoln

Andrew Johnson (1865 – 1869)

- He was an apprentice tailor at age 14 and later moved to Tennessee to open his own tailor shop. Using these skills, he made all of his own suits as president.
- He was the first president to be impeached. He violated the Tenure of Office Act by firing the Secretary of State.
- He was the only Southerner to retain his Senate seat upon secession.
- He never attended school and taught himself how to read.
- People thought he had a drinking problem because he slurred his words at his inauguration. It turned out he had indeed imbibed whiskey before the speech, but did so to combat the symptoms of Typhoid fever (from which he recovered).

INGREDIENTS

2 ½ ounces Russian Standard vodka
½ ounce Martini & Rossi dry vermouth
½ ounce spicy olive juice
¼ teaspoon extra virgin olive oil
Garnish: Sable & Rosenfeld tipsy onions (3) and Mezzetta jalapeño stuffed olives (2) (skewered on toothpicks)

PREPARATION

Combine all ingredients in a cocktail shaker with ice and shake well. Strain into a martini glass. Garnish with onions and olives.

1865	1865	1865	1867	1867
John Wilkes Booth was shot and killed in a tobacco barn in Virginia		The Ku Klux Klan was founded in Pulaski, Tennessee		Alfred Nobel patented dynamite in England
	The first rail of the Transcontinental Railroad was laid in Omaha, Nebraska		The U.S. purchased Alaska from Russia for $7.2 million; the deal was known as Seward's Folly	

Honest conversation is my courage;
the Constitution is my guide.
–Andrew Johnson

Ulysses S. Grant (1869 – 1877)

- He was the Union general who led the U.S. to victory over the Confederacy even though he could not stand the sight of blood.
- "S" does not stand for anything—a clerical error was made in his nomination to attend West Point. His actual name was Hiram Ulysses Grant.
- He was supposed to be in Lincoln's theater box the night of the assassination.
- He dismantled the Ku Klux Klan during his presidency (they later regrouped).
- Both he and his wife Julia are interred at Grant's Tomb (the largest mausoleum in North America).

INGREDIENTS

5 ounces Kirkland Champagne brut
1 ounce Twisted Alchemy
   blood orange juice

PREPARATION

Pour Champagne into champagne flute and top off with blood orange juice.

The Transcontinental Railroad was completed		The 15th Amendment granted voting rights (to men) regardless of race		Ethiopia prevailed in a war with Egypt over access to the Nile basin
1869	**1869**	**1870**	**1871**	**1876**
	The Knights of Labor (first major American labor union) was founded		The Great Chicago Fire burned for three days, leaving more than 100,000 homeless	

The art of war is simple enough. Find out where your enemy is. Get at him as soon as you can. Strike him as hard as you can, and keep moving on.
–Ulysses S. Grant

Rutherford B. Hayes (1877 – 1881)

- He was nicknamed "Rutherfraud" after he won a heavily disputed election. He lost the popular vote (the first of four Republican presidents to do so) and won the electoral college by only one vote (with 20 of the votes disputed).
- He was also called "Granny Hayes" because he did not drink, smoke, or gamble.
- He was the first president to have a telephone in the White House. It was installed by Alexander Graham Bell himself.
- He kept many pets at the White House—Jersey cows, five kittens, five dogs, five birds, a goat, and several horses.
- He and Mrs. Hayes hosted the first Easter Egg Roll on the White House lawn.

INGREDIENTS

1 ½ ounces Aviation gin
Belvoir Elderflower & Rose
 lemonade
Garnish: lemon twist

PREPARATION

Pour gin into ice-filled rocks glass. Top off with lemonade. Garnish with lemon twist.

1877	1877	1877	1879	1880
Railroad employees, unhappy over cut wages, began what came to be known as the Great Railroad Strike of 1877		The Compromise of 1877 ended the Reconstruction Era		The president pronounced the necessity of creating an American-controlled canal in Panama
	Thomas Edison invented the tin foil phonograph		Thomas Edison filed for a patent for an electric lamp	

One of the tests of the civilization of people is the
treatment of its criminals.

–Rutherford B. Hayes

James Garfield (1881 – 1881)

- He was ambidextrous and could write in Greek with one hand and Latin with the other at the same time.
- He was assassinated about six months into his presidency; his spinal column is displayed at the National Museum of Health and Medicine.
- He was the only president that was an ordained minister.
- His favorite food was squirrel soup.
- He never pursued the presidency. He became a compromise candidate after there was a stalemate between three other candidates.

INGREDIENTS

1 ½ ounces Barbayanni ouzo
½ ounce Disaronno amaretto
½ ounce Twisted Alchemy
    passion fruit juice
Scrappy's orange bitters (2 dashes)
8 fresh raspberries
Garnish: 2 fresh raspberries

PREPARATION

Purée passion fruit juice, raspberries and bitters in blender until smooth. Combine ouzo and amaretto in cocktail shaker with ice and shake well. Pour ouzo and amaretto into an ice-filled rocks glass. Pour rasberry purée over cocktail to seep through ice. Garnish with rasberries

Garfield was not president long enough for anything to really happen!

1881

The truth will set you free,
but first it will make you miserable.
–James Garfield

Chester A. Arthur (1881 – 1885)

- He was nicknamed "Elegant Arthur" because he owned more than 80 pairs of pants.
- He sold off 24 wagonloads of America's historic relics, including a pair of Lincoln's pants, to help pay the costs to redecorate the White House—a project led by Louis Comfort Tiffany.
- He was the first president to have a personal valet.
- He had never been elected to any office when he became president upon Garfield's death.
- In an early Birther conspiracy, his detractors tried to convince the public he was born outside the U.S. because his father had lived in Ireland and Canada before he was born. He was actually born in Vermont.

INGREDIENTS

2 ounces Grands Domaines VS cognac

1 ounce Disaronno amaretto

Zest of ½ lime

PREPARATION

Combine cognac and amarreto in an ice-filled rocks glass. Sprinkle lime zest on top. Optional: serve with Coconut and Chocolate Rum Ball

1881	1883	1883	1883	1885
Tsar Alexander II of the Russian Empire was assassinated		The Brooklyn Bridge opened as the first "fixed" means of crossing the East River		The Washington Monument was dedicated following a 23-year halt in construction due largely to the American Civil War
	France colonized Indochina, including modern-day Vietnam, Laos and Cambodia		The Orient Express commenced passenger service between Paris and Constantinople	

Where you stand depends on where you sit.
–Chester A. Arthur

Grover Cleveland (1885 – 1889)

- He became the legal guardian of his law partner's daughter when she was 11. He married her 10 years later at the White House, making her the youngest first lady in history.
- He was the first president to marry in the White House and was only the second president to assume the presidency while single.
- He was a distant relative of the person the city of Cleveland was named after.
- His real first name was Stephen; Grover was his middle name.
- He was nicknamed "Big Steve" and was the first morbidly obese president.

INGREDIENTS

4 ounces Zing Zang bloody mary mix
Temptress Imperial Milk stout
1 teaspoon chopped chipotle pepper in adobo sauce
Demitris Bacon Rim Shot
1 Lime
Garnish: pickled okra and lime wedge

PREPARATION

Cut lime in half and rub cut side over rim of highball glass. Dip glass rim into Bacon Rim Shot. Fill glass with ice and add bloody mary mix. Add chipotle pepper and stir. Top off with stout. Garnish with pickled okra and lime wedge.

1886	1886	1886	1887	1889

The statue "Liberty Enlightening the World," a gift from France, was dedicated as the "Statue of Liberty"

The Klondike gold rush began in Alaska

The Eiffel Tower, then the tallest man-made structure in the world, was inaugurated

A bombing took place in Haymarket Square in Chicago

The flooding of the Yellow River in China killed over 900,000 people

Though the people support the government,
the government should not support the people.
–Grover Cleveland

Benjamin Harrison (1889 – 1893)

- The grandson of President William Henry Harrison, he was known to be stiff in demeanor, earning the nickname "Human Iceberg."
- He was the first president to have electricity in the White House. It was rumored that fear of electrocution contributed to his stiffness.
- During his administration, Congress appropriated $1 billion in annual spending for the first time.
- He was the only incumbent president defeated by a former president.
- He was featured on the $5 national bank note, one of eight presidents to have been on the five-dollar bill.

INGREDIENTS

1 ½ ounces Farmer's Botanical gin
6 ounces Taylors lemon
    and orange tea
1 ounce blood orange juice
½ ounce lemon juice
½ teaspoon honey
Garnish: 5 lavender flowers

PREPARATION

Brew tea and chill. Combine all ingredients in a cocktail shaker and shake well. Strain into ice-filled highball glass. Sprinke lavender flowers on top.

1890	1890	1891	1891	1892	
The Sherman Antitrust Act was passed to outlaw monopolistic business practices		Oscar Wilde published the controversial novel *The Picture of Dorian Gray*		Ellis Island opened up as a federal immigration inspection station	
	The Wounded Knee Massacre resulted in the deaths of 146 Lakota Sioux		The Ninth Circuit Court of Appeals was established in California		

Great lives never go out; they go on.
–Benjamin Harrison

Grover Cleveland (1893 – 1897)

- He was the only president to serve nonconsecutive terms.
- A third party, the Populist Party, helped him get elected by taking 8% of the popular vote.
- Before becoming a lawyer, he was a teacher at the New York Institute for the Blind in Manhattan.
- He was the governor of New York before becoming president and was known as "Uncle Jumbo."
- He avoided serving in the military during the Civil War by paying a $300 fee.

INGREDIENTS

1 ounce Havana Club Selección Maestro Cuban rum
1 ounce Havana Club Añejo Clásico Puerto Rican rum
½ ounce Grand Marnier
½ ounce lime juice
½ ounce Liber & Co. orgeat syrup
Garnish: 3 fresh raspberries

PREPARATION

Combine all ingredient in a cocktail shaker with ice and shake well. Strain into an ice-filled highball glass. Garnish with raspberries.

The Panic of 1893 sparked a three-year economic depression		A protest in Cleveland turned into the May Day Riots, sparking a wave of other protests and strikes across the country		Marconi sent and received Morse code-based radio signals	
1893	**1893**	**1894**	**1895**	**1896**	
	The World's Fair took place in Chicago		Cuba rebelled against Spanish rule		

Honor Lies in Honest Toil.
–Grover Cleveland

William McKinley (1897 – 1901)

- He considered carnations to be his good luck charm and always wore one in his lapel.
- He was the first president to ride in an automobile while in office.
- He was the first president to use a telephone to campaign.
- He was the only president between Andrew Johnson and Woodrow Wilson who was clean-shaven.
- He had a pet parrot named "Washington Post."

INGREDIENTS

2 ounces Jack Daniels rye whiskey
1 ounce Cocchi sweet vermouth
1 teaspoon Luxardo cherry liqueur
S. Pellegrino Blood Orange & Black
    Raspberry sparkling water
Garnish: lemon wedge

PREPARATION

Combine rye whiskey, sweet vermouth and cherry liqueur in a cocktail shaker with ice and shake well. Strain into an ice-filled highball glass. Top off with sparkling water. Garnish with lemon wedge.

Nikola Tesla invented the induction (Tesla) coil and the transmission of electricity via alternating current

The Boxer Rebellion began in China as a peasant uprising to drive out foreigners

The Galveston Hurricane killed 8,000 people

1897   **1898**   **1899**   **1900**   **1900**

The Spanish-American War began following an explosion aboard the USS Maine in Havana Harbor, Cuba

The Gold Standard Act eliminated silver redemption for paper money

In the time of darkest defeat, victory may be nearest.
–William McKinley

Theodore Roosevelt (1901 – 1909)

- His mother and first wife both died on Valentine's Day in 1884.
- He was once shot while giving a speech but continued talking until the 90-minute speech was finished.
- After news got out that he refused to shoot a bear cub on a hunting trip as president, a toymaker started making "Teddy Bears."
- He was the first president to win a Nobel Peace Prize (for his role in the Treaty of Portsmouth).
- He was blind in one eye because of a boxing injury sustained while in the White House. He stopped boxing and switched to jiu-jitsu.

INGREDIENTS

2 ounces Knob Creek
    bourbon whiskey
10 mint leaves
3 strawberries
2 pieces crystallized ginger
Club soda
Garnish: crystallized ginger, mint
    leaf and strawberry (skewered
    on a cocktail stick)

PREPARATION

Purée whiskey, mint leaves, strawberries and one piece of crystallized ginger in a blender. Strain into an ice-filled rocks glass. Top off with club soda. Place garnish diagonally on rim of glass.

1902	1904	1906	1906	1908
The Wright brothers flew the first plane not powered by wind		An estimated 7.9 magnitude Earthquake in San Francisco killed 3,000 people		Henry Ford introduced the "Model T" automobile
	The Russo-Japanese War began		Finland became the first European nation to grant women the right to vote	

*Keep your eyes on the stars,
and your feet on the ground.*
–Theodore Roosevelt

William Howard Taft (1909 – 1913)

- Toy makers believed that Teddy Bears would fade out and created "Billy Possums" after Taft ate a huge possum for dinner one night. They never really caught on.
- He was the first president to throw out the first pitch of baseball season.
- He was the first president to own a car, converting the White House stables into a garage.
- He is the only president to serve as Chief Justice of the Supreme Court.
- He was the first president buried at Arlington National Cemetery.

INGREDIENTS

1 ounce Casa Dragones
    tequila blanco
Kirkland Champagne brut
½ chopped peach
Garnish: peach slice

PREPARATION

Muddle peach in cocktail shaker. Add tequila and ice and shake well. Strain into an ice-filled rocks glass. Top off with champagne. Garnish with peach slice.

The decade-long Mexican Revolution (and Civil War) began

The Chinese Revolution overthrew the Qing Dynasty, leading to the Republic of China

The 16th Amendment gave Congress the right to collect income taxes directly

1910   **1910**   **1911**   **1912**   **1913**

The Postal Savings System was created to bring in the unbanked

The *Titanic* sunk off the coast of Newfoundland

*We are all imperfect. We can never
expect perfect government.*
–William Howard Taft

Woodrow Wilson (1913 – 1921)

- He remained in office for two years after experiencing a series of strokes believed to have been caused by the Spanish Flu. The length and severity of his illness while in office eventually led to the 25th Amendment dealing with the incapacitation of a president while in office.
- He was the last president to arrive at his inauguration in a horse-drawn carriage.
- He put the first Jewish Justice on the Supreme Court (Louis Brandeis).
- He is the only president to be buried in Washington, D.C. (in the Washington National Cathedral).
- He never officially addressed the Spanish Flu pandemic with the nation.

INGREDIENTS

¾ ounce Monkey Shoulder Scotch whisky
¾ ounce Cocchi sweet vermouth
¾ ounce Bellini Amaro Delle Terme
¾ ounce Luxardo Cherry liqueur
¾ ounce Twisted Alchemy blood orange juice
Garnish: blood orange wheel

PREPARATION

Combine all ingredientes in a cocktail shaker with ice and shake well. Strain into an ice-filed highball glass. Garnish with blood orange wheel.

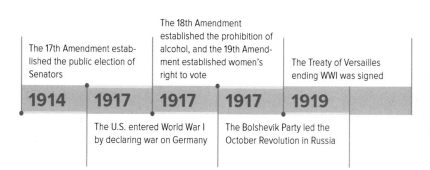

The 17th Amendment established the public election of Senators

The 18th Amendment established the prohibition of alcohol, and the 19th Amendment established women's right to vote

The Treaty of Versailles ending WWI was signed

| 1914 | 1917 | 1917 | 1917 | 1919 |

The U.S. entered World War I by declaring war on Germany

The Bolshevik Party led the October Revolution in Russia

*Friendship is the only cement that will ever
hold the world together.*
–Woodrow Wilson

Warren G. Harding (1921 – 1923)

- He had a number of extramarital affairs, including one with a close friend of his wife and another with a woman who identified him in a book as the father of her daughter (he was).
- He officially ended World War I (the U.S. Senate had not previously ratified the Treaty of Versailles).
- He liked to play poker and once lost a set of White House china in a poker game.
- He wore size 19 shoes, making his feet the largest of any president.
- He was a newspaper reporter before he became a politician.

INGREDIENTS

2 ounces Wolfhound
   Irish whiskey
3 ounces McClures Spicy
   Pickles Spears pickle juice
1 ounce lime juice
½ teaspoon honey
½ teaspoon Sriracha sauce
Garnish: pinch of paprika

PREPARATION

Combine all ingredients in a cocktail shaker with ice and shake well. Strain into an ice-filled highball glass. Sprinkle paprika on top.

The U.S. officially opposed entry to the League of Nations		Harding pardoned Eugene V. Debs of his 1918 conviction of sedition		The Union of Soviet Socialist Republics (U.S.S.R.) was created
1921	**1921**	**1921**	**1922**	**1922**
	The Teapot Dome Scandal exposed bribery between Big Oil and the Harding Administration		The Irish Free State (Republic of Ireland) was established	

Every student has the ability to be a successful learner.
–Warren G. Harding

Calvin Coolidge (1923 – 1929)

- He had a morning ritual of having someone rub Vaseline on his head while he ate breakfast.
- He was the only president born on the Fourth of July.
- He was sworn into office by his own father. He was visiting his father in Vermont when Harding died, and his father, who was a notary public, officiated.
- He was the first sitting president to visit Cuba.
- He had two pet raccoons while in the White House.

INGREDIENTS

1 ½ ounces Maker's Mark bourbon whiskey
1 ½ ounces Royal Tokaji 5 puttonyos aszú
1 ½ ounces Twisted Alchemy passion fruit juice
Garnish: lime wheel

PREPARATION

Combine all ingredients in a cocktail shaker with ice and shake well. Strain into an ice-filled wine glass. Garnish with lime wheel.

1925	1925	1927	1927	1929
The Scopes Monkey Trial opened the Modernist/Fundamentalist debate		Charles Lindbergh made the first nonstop transatlantic flight		The Lateran Treaty established Vatican City as an independent city-state from Fascist Italy
	The Pahlavi Dynasty established the final monarchy of Iran		The first talking motion picture (*The Jazz Singer*) was produced	

If you see ten troubles coming down the road, you can be sure that nine will run into the ditch before they reach you.
–Calvin Coolidge

Herbert Hoover (1929 – 1933)

- He and his wife spoke Mandarin when they wanted to have a private conversation in the White House. They had previously lived in China.
- He was a member of Stanford University's inaugural class.
- His son had two pet alligators while living in the White House.
- He became rich as a leading mining engineer and had a net worth of more than $75 million in current dollars.
- He wanted his servants to be invisible, requiring them to hide in closets when he entered a room or risk being fired.

INGREDIENTS

2 ounces Absolut vodka
½ ounce Martini & Rossi
    dry vermouth
Lemon
Garnish: Haywards Traditional
    onion and lemon wheel

PREPARATION

Combine vodka, dry vermouth, 3 large pieces of lemon peel and the juice from ½ of the lemon in an ice-filled cocktail shaker and shake well. Strain into a martini glass. Garnish with onion and lemon wheel.

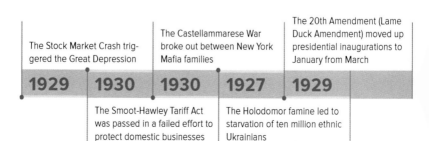

The Stock Market Crash triggered the Great Depression

The Castellammarese War broke out between New York Mafia families

The 20th Amendment (Lame Duck Amendment) moved up presidential inaugurations to January from March

1929 **1930** **1930** **1927** **1929**

The Smoot-Hawley Tariff Act was passed in a failed effort to protect domestic businesses and farmers.

The Holodomor famine led to starvation of ten million ethnic Ukrainians

*Older men declare war. But it is the youth
that must fight and die.*
–Herbert Hoover

Franklin D. Roosevelt (1933 – 1945)

- He was obsessed with his dog, Fala, and even made him an honorary Army private during WWII.
- He appointed Frances Perkins as Secretary of Labor, the first woman to hold a Cabinet-level position.
- His wife, Eleanor, was actually his fifth cousin and already had the Roosevelt name at the time of their marriage.
- He was superstitious about the number 13, refusing to dine in a group of 13 or to travel on the 13th of any month.
- While he was widely believed to have had polio, more recent research suggests that he may actually have had Guillain-Barre Syndrome.

INGREDIENTS

1 ounce The Lone Star gin
1 ounce Campari
1 ounce Cocchi sweet vermouth
1 ounce Twisted Alchemy
     blood orange juice
Garnish: blood orange wheel

PREPARATION

Combine all ingredients in a cocktail shaker with ice and shake well. Strain into an ice-filled rocks glass. Place blood orange wheel over ice.

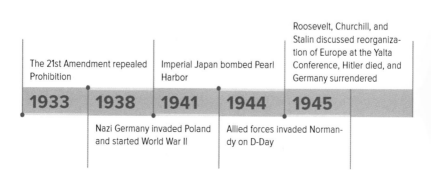

The 21st Amendment repealed Prohibition		Imperial Japan bombed Pearl Harbor		Roosevelt, Churchill, and Stalin discussed reorganization of Europe at the Yalta Conference, Hitler died, and Germany surrendered
1933	**1938**	**1941**	**1944**	**1945**
	Nazi Germany invaded Poland and started World War II		Allied forces invaded Normandy on D-Day	

The only thing we have to fear is fear itself.
–Franklin D. Roosevelt

Harry S. Truman (1945 – 1953)

- A placard on his desk stating "The Buck Stops Here" signified his belief that the president must make decisions and accept ultimate responsibility for them.
- His middle name is actually "S." Because his parents could not agree on a middle name, they settled on "S" as a tribute to his two grandfathers, both of whose names began with the letter.
- His second inauguration was the first to be nationally televised.
- He was the only president of the 1900s who did not attend college.
- He met his wife, Bess, in school when he was six years old.

INGREDIENTS

1 ounce Johnnie Walker Red Label Scotch whisky
½ ounce Luxardo apricot liqueur
¾ ounce Campari
½ ounce Cointreau orange liqueur
1 ounce apple cider
Garnish: two lime wedges

PREPARATION

Combine all ingredients in a cocktail shaker with ice and shake well. Strain into an ice-filled copper mule mug. Garnish with lime wedges.

The U.S. dropped atomic bombs on Hiroshima and Nagasaki, Allied leaders met at the Potsdam Conference, and Japan surrendered, officially ending World War II

The U.S. introduced the Marshall Plan to reconstruct Western Europe

The Korean War began, and separately but relatedly, McCarthy started the Witch Hunts for communists

1945   **1945**   **1947**   **1949**   **1950**

The United Nations was established and the Cold War set in

The NATO Treaty was signed as a Western bulwark against Soviet power

A pessimist is one who makes difficulties of his opportunities and on optimist is one who makes opportunities of his difficulties.
–Harry S. Truman

Dwight D. Eisenhower (1953 – 1961)

- He renamed FDR's presidential "Shangri-la" retreat "Camp David" (after his father and grandson), reasoning the previous name was "just a little too fancy for a Kansas farm boy."
- He never saw active duty or combat although he was in the military for 35 years.
- He banished squirrels from the White House grounds because they were ruining his putting green.
- He was the first president to ride in a helicopter, as the Secret Service thought that he would be safer in helicopters than limousines for short trips.
- His birth name was David Dwight Eisenhower, but his mother transposed the name to avoid confusion with his father.

INGREDIENTS

1 ounce Hirsch Reserve bourbon whiskey
1 ounce Absente absinthe
½ ounce Martini & Rossi dry vermouth
Scrappy's orange bitters (3 dashes)

PREPARATION

Combine all ingredients in a cocktail shaker with ice and shake well. Strain into an ice-filled rocks glass.

1953	1954	1955	1957	1959
The Korean War ended in an armistice		The Vietnam War sparked conflict throughout Indochina		Cuba falls to the Movement, becoming, under Fidel Castro, the first Communist state in the Western Hemisphere
	The Brown v. Board of Education decision ruled against segregation		The Soviet Union launched *Sputnik I*, the first satellite to orbit Earth	

Plans are nothing; planning is everything.
–Dwight D. Eisenhower

John F. Kennedy (1961 – 1963)

- He was the first president who was a Boy Scout (he was also the youngest person ever elected president at age 43).
- He won the Pulitzer Prize in history for his book *Profiles in Courage*.
- He and all nine of his siblings received $1 million checks (about $20 million today) on their 21st birthdays.
- He suffered from poor health throughout his life, and had received last rites three times before his presidency (he was also the first Catholic president).
- Marilyn Monroe sang "Happy Birthday" to him at his 45th birthday party at Madison Square Garden.

INGREDIENTS

2 ounces Malecón Reserve Superior aged rum
2 ounces mango juice
1 ounce lime juice
½ ounce simple syrup
Garnish: pinch of ground cinnamon

PREPARATION

Combine all ingredients in a cocktail shaker with ice and shake well. Strain into an ice-filled highball glass. Sprinkle cinnamon on top.

The Peace Corps was created to "promote a better understanding of Americans"		The Cuban Missile Crisis brings the world to the brink of nuclear holocaust		More than 200,000 take part in the March on Washington for Jobs and Freedom
1961	**1961**	**1962**	**1962**	**1963**
	The Bay of Pigs Invasion failed to overthrow Castro		John Glenn became the first American to orbit Earth	

A child miseducated is a child lost.
–John F. Kennedy

Lyndon B. Johnson (1963 – 1969)

- During WWII, he boarded the Wabash Cannonball bomber for a mission in the South Pacific. He deboarded the plane for the bathroom before takeoff. The plane took off without him and ultimately crashed, killing everyone on board.
- He had a domineering personality and was known for the "Johnson Treatment," an aggressive coercion of powerful politicians to advance legislation.
- He asked his wife to marry him on their first date and she accepted 10 weeks later.
- He was the first president sworn in by a woman, Federal District Judge Sarah Hughes.
- He liked to give away electric toothbrushes with the presidential seal so that people thought about him when they woke up and when they went to sleep.

INGREDIENTS

1 ounce Tanteo Blanco tequila
½ ounce Tanteo Jalapeño tequila
¼ ounce Aperol
Lime sour slush
Topo Chico
Garnish: lime wheel

PREPARATION

Freeze lime sour in globe ice tray for 3 hours. Place slush in highball glass. Combine tequilas in cocktail shaker with ice and shake well. Strain into the highball glass. Top off with Topo Chico. Add Aperol. Garnish with lime wheel.

The Beatles arrived in New York City for their first U.S. tour		The Selma Freedom March took place in Alabama, and Malcolm X was assassinated		Dr. Martin Luther King, Jr., and Robert Kennedy were assassinated
1964	**1964**	**1965**	**1967**	**1968**
	The Civil Rights Act codified equal treatment of Americans		Israel defeated a league of Arab states in the Six-Day War	

*Yesterday is not ours to recover,
but tomorrow is ours to win or lose.*
–Lyndon B. Johnson

Richard M. Nixon (1969 – 1974)

- He is the only president to resign from office (following the Watergate scandal).
- He loved bowling and had a one-lane alley put in the basement of the White House.
- He is the first president to visit a nation not recognized by the U.S., visiting China in 1972.
- He could play five musical instruments—the piano, saxophone, clarinet, accordion, and violin.
- He wrote ten best-selling books on domestic and international affairs.

PREPARATION

Combine all ingredients in an ice-filled pitcher and stir vigorously. Pour into ice-filled tiki glasses. Garnish with pineapple spike and umbrella.

INGREDIENTS

(4 servings)

1 ½ ounces Goslings Black Seal Bermuda rum

1 ½ ounces Brugal Añejo Superior rum

1 ½ ounces coconut rum

½ ounce 151 overproof Demarara rum

1 ounce Leblon cachaça

1 ½ ounces Luxardo cherry liqueur

2 ounces Grand Marnier

3 ounces orange juice

3 ounces pineapple juice

1 ounce Liber & Co. orgeat syrup

Garnish: pineapple spike, orange wedge, lime wheel and Luxardo maraschino cherry (last three garnishes skewered on paper umbrella)

1970	1972	1972	1973	1973
Hafez al-Assad led the coup to take over Syria and establish power		The U.S. and the U.S.S.R. signed the Strategic Arms Limitation Treaty (SALT) and Anti-Ballistic Missile Treaty		The Roe v. Wade ruling by the Supreme Court established pro-choice reproductive rights in the U.S.
	The Munich Massacre resulted in the deaths of 11 Israeli athletes at the Summer Olympics		The Vietnam War ended with the fall of Saigon to Communist North Vietnam	

The finest steel has to go through the hottest fire.
—Richard M. Nixon

Gerald R. Ford (1974 – 1977)

- He is the only president never elected to either the office of president or vice president.
- His birth name was Leslie Lynch King, Jr. The Ford name came from his mother's second husband.
- Two assassination attempts were made on his life, 17 days apart, and each by a woman.
- He was once a male model and had a photo spread in *Look* magazine with his then-girlfriend Phyllis Brown.
- He and his wife played themselves in an episode of the TV soap opera *Dynasty* in a charity ball scene with Blake and Cristal Carrington.

INGREDIENTS

1 ounce Drambuie
2 ounces apple juice
½ ounce Liber & Co. Fiery
    ginger syrup
Henry Hotspur's Hard
    Pressed cider
1 ounce ginger ale
Ground cinnamon
Garnish: apple slice and
    cinnamon stick

PREPARATION

Wet the rim of a mason jar with water and dip rim into ground cinnamon. Fill mason jar with ice. Combine Drambuie, apple juice, ginger ale and ginger syrup in a cocktail shaker with ice and shake well. Strain into the mason jar and top off with cider. Garnish with apple slice. Place cinnammon stick on rim of glass to stir.

1974	1975	1975	1976	1977
The "Whip Inflation Now – WIN" program was announced to combat stagflation		Pol Pot led the Khmer Rouge to takeover Cambodia		The Concorde launched commercial service between Europe and the U.S.
	Upon Franco's death, Juan Carlos I was crowned King of Spain		A 7.5 magnitude earthquake killed nearly 250,000 people in Tangshan, China	

Tell the truth, work hard, and come to dinner on time.
–Gerald R. Ford

Jimmy Carter (1977 – 1981)

- He (uncharacteristically) gave an interview to *Playboy* while running for president and admitted that "he looked upon a lot of women with lust."
- He is the only graduate of the U.S. Naval Academy elected president.
- He was the first president to be born in a hospital.
- He was nominated for five Grammy Awards and won three.
- He did not like the pageantry of the presidency; he sold the presidential yacht and banned the playing of "Hail to the Chief" during appearances.

INGREDIENTS

1 ½ ounces Skatter Brain peanut butter whiskey
¾ ounce Flor de Caña Añejo Oro 4-years rum
½ ounce pineapple juice
½ ounce orange juice
Garnish: lemon wedge

PREPARATION

Combine all ingredients in a cocktail shaker with ice and shake well. Strain into an ice-filled rocks glass. Garnish with lemon wedge. Optional: serve with peanuts.

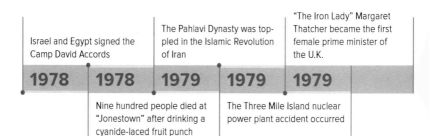

1978	1978	1979	1979	1979
Israel and Egypt signed the Camp David Accords		The Pahlavi Dynasty was toppled in the Islamic Revolution of Iran		"The Iron Lady" Margaret Thatcher became the first female prime minister of the U.K.
	Nine hundred people died at "Jonestown" after drinking a cyanide-laced fruit punch		The Three Mile Island nuclear power plant accident occurred	

America did not invent human rights.
Human rights invented America.
–Jimmy Carter

Ronald Reagan (1981 – 1989)

- He was almost strangled by a chimp during the filming of *Bedtime for Bonzo*, when Bonzo started pulling at his tie and would not let go.
- "Dutch" was his lifelong nickname given to him shortly after birth by his father who referred to him as a "fat little Dutchman."
- He was an FBI informant along with his first wife, Jane Wyman, providing tips on suspected Communist activity in Hollywood.
- Shirley Temple considered him to be one of her best on-screen kissers.
- As president, he regularly consulted with astrologer Joan Quigley before making decisions and scheduling big events.

INGREDIENTS

1 ½ ounces Ketel One Peach & Orange Blossom vodka
½ ounce Twisted Alchemy Persian lime sour juice
Kirkland Champagne brut

PREPARATION

Combine vodka and Persian lime sour juice in a cocktail shaker with ice and shake well. Strain into a martini glass and top off with Champagne.

1982	1983	1985	1986	1989
Argentina invaded the Falkland Islands and was defeated by British forces in 74 days		The Iran-Contra scandal revealed illegal U.S. arms sales to the Iranian regime		The Berlin Wall fell and most Communist governments across Eastern Europe collapsed
	Islamic Jihad killed 299 American and French troops in the Beirut barracks bombing		The Space Shuttle *Challenger* disintegrated on live TV, 73 seconds after launch	

*When you can't make them see the light,
make them feel the heat.*
–Ronald Reagan

George H. W. Bush (1989 – 1993)

- He inspired the Japanese word "Bushusuru," which means "to do the Bush thing," after he became ill and vomited on the Japanese prime minister at a dinner.
- In college he was captain of the Yale University baseball team and played in the first two College World Series. He was also a member of the cheerleading squad.
- He was married for 73 years to Barbara Pierce Bush, making him the second longest-married president to date (behind the Carters).
- He loved socks and told NPR about them, "The louder, the brighter, the crazier the pattern the better."
- He is the only president who lived to see the commissioning of an aircraft carrier named in his honor.

INGREDIENTS

1 ½ ounces Iwai Mars Japanese whisky
¼ ounce Libor & Co. ginger syrup
Fever-Tree sparkling lemon
Garnish: lemon twist and lemon wheel

PREPARATION

Combine whisky and ginger syrup in a cocktail shaker with ice and shake well. Strain into an ice-filled rocks glass. Top off with sparkling lemon. Garnish with lemon twist and lemon wheel. Optional: serve with wasabi peas and crystallized ginger.

The Exxon *Valdez* oil spill in Alaska became one of the greatest environmental catastrophes in history		The Tiananmen Square Massacre occurred in Beijing and, in an unrelated event, Germany reunified		Riots in Los Angeles killed 53 people following the acquittal of three LAPD officers in the beating of Rodney King
1989	**1989**	**1990**	**1991**	**1992**
	The U.S. invaded Panama, ousting dictator Mañuel Noriega		The First Gulf War dubbed "Operation Desert Storm" began following Iraq's invasion of Kuwait	

I have opinions of my own — strong opinions — but I don't always agree with them.
—George H.W. Bush

Bill Clinton (1993 – 2001)

- He and George H. W. Bush are the only consecutive presidents that are left-handed (they are also both 6'2" tall).
- He has won two Grammys (one for Best Spoken Word Album and the other for Best Spoken Word Album for Children).
- He is the only president that was a Rhodes Scholar.
- He shook hands with John F. Kennedy when he was 16 years old, just four months before Kennedy's death.
- He was so impressed with Dr. Martin Luther King Jr.'s "I Have a Dream" speech that he memorized it right after it was given.

INGREDIENTS

1 ½ ounces Hendrick's gin
½ ounce Domaine de Canton ginger liqueur
Howling Gourds Pumpkin ale
1 ounce apple cider
½ teaspoon fresh ginger
Garnish: ground ginger

PREPARATION

Freeze apple cider in globe ice tray for six hours. Place ice cube in highball glass. Combine gin, ginger liqueur, apple cider and fresh ginger in a cocktail shaker with ice and shake well. Strain into the highball glass. Top off with ale. Sprinkle ground ginger on top.

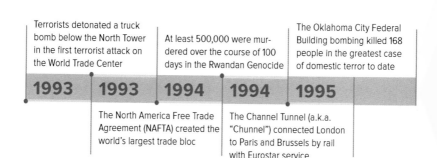

Terrorists detonated a truck bomb below the North Tower in the first terrorist attack on the World Trade Center

At least 500,000 were murdered over the course of 100 days in the Rwandan Genocide

The Oklahoma City Federal Building bombing killed 168 people in the greatest case of domestic terror to date

1993 | **1993** | **1994** | **1994** | **1995**

The North America Free Trade Agreement (NAFTA) created the world's largest trade bloc

The Channel Tunnel (a.k.a. "Chunnel") connected London to Paris and Brussels by rail with Eurostar service

Sometimes when people are under stress, they hate to think, and it's the time when they most need to think.
–Bill Clinton

George W. Bush (2001 – 2009)

- He is the only president to run a marathon, completing the Houston Marathon in a time of 3:44:52.
- He is the only president to have twins (daughters Jenna and Barbara).
- He is the only president to hold an MBA (he earned it from Harvard).
- He had the highest approval rating of any president in history (86% in October 2001) in the aftermath of his handling of the 9/11 attacks.
- He was part owner of the Texas Rangers for five years, and sold his stake for roughly fourteen times the price he paid ($800,000/$14.9 million).

INGREDIENTS

1 ounce Tito's vodka
1 ½ ounces Lillet rosé
Topo Chico
Garnish: mint sprig

PREPARATION

Combine vodka and Lillet in cocktail shaker filled with ice and shake well. Strain into an ice-filled highball glass. Top off with Topo Chico. Garnish with mint sprig.

2001	2003	2003	2005	2008
The World Trade Center was attacked by terrorists on 9/11, sparking the "War on Terror"		Saddam Hussein (Ace of Spades) was captured and subsequently executed		A run-up in speculative debt, led by toxic mortgages, triggered a financial crisis and the beginning of the Great Recession
	The Space Shuttle *Columbia* broke up on reentry over Palestine, Texas		Hurricane *Katrina* devastated Louisiana and the Gulf Coast, causing over 1,800 deaths and $125 billion in damage	

Faith crosses every border and touches every heart in every nation.
–George W. Bush

Barack Obama (2009 – 2017)

- He was nicknamed "O'Bomber" in high school for his basketball skills.
- He is the first president born in Hawaii and thus the first to be born outside the continental U.S.
- When president his secret service codename was "Renegade," and First Lady Michelle Obama's was "Renaissance."
- He has received two Grammy Awards, both for Spoken Word Album of the Year.
- He had to retake the oath of office the day after his first inauguration because he made a wording mistake.

INGREDIENTS

2 ounces Tanteo Habanero tequila
1 ounce Cointreau
½ ounce Chambord
2 ounces pineapple juice
Garnish – 3 blackberries and 2 rasberries (skewered on a cocktail stick)

PREPARATION

Combine tequila, Cointreau and pineapple juice in a cocktail shaker with ice and shake well. Strain into an ice-filled wine glass. Pour Chambord over mixture. Place garnish on rim of glass.

The "Arab Spring" movement started in Tunisia following the self-immolation of a street vendor in protest of government harassment

Pope Benedict XVI resigned and Pope Francis became the 266th pope of the Roman Catholic Church

The Russian Federation annexed Crimea from Ukraine and deployed clandestine forces to Eastern Ukraine

2010 2011 2013 2013 2014

U.S. troops kill *Al Qaeda* leader and 9/11 mastermind Osama bin Laden

The Boston Marathon bombing killed three spectators and severely injured 260 others

If you're walking down the right path and you're willing to keep walking, eventually you'll make progress.
–Barack Obama

Donald J. Trump (2017 –)

- He has a star on the Hollywood Walk of Fame, which he received for producing and starring in the reality TV show *The Apprentice* where his catchphrase famously became "You're Fired!"
- He is a germophobe who does not like to shake hands or touch doorknobs or elevator buttons.
- He doesn't drink or smoke because his older brother struggled with addiction, but he did briefly have his own Vodka brand.
- He is the first billionaire to become president.
- He has made cameo appearances in 12 films and 14 TV series. He has been nominated for two Emmy Awards, but has never won.

INGREDIENTS

2 ounces 151 overproof
    Demarara rum
1 ounce mango juice
1 ounce orange juice
Topo Chico
Garnish: orange wheel

PREPARATION

Combine rum, mango juice and orange juice in a cocktail shaker with ice and shake well. Pour into ice-filled highball glass. Top off with Topo Chico. Garnish with orange wheel. Optional: serve with Goldfish, Cheetos or other orange-colored snack.

A shooter killed 59 people and wounded 412 from the 32nd floor of the Mandalay Bay Hotel in Las Vegas

A large fire nearly destroyed Notre Dame Cathedral in Paris

The COVID-19 health pandemic spread across the globe; the resulting economic collapse disrupted the world and delayed the Tokyo Summer Olympic Games

2017 | **2018** | **2019** | **2020** | **2020**

The leaders of the U.S. and North Korea met for the first time in history

BREXIT, the United Kingdom's withdrawal from the European Union, officially began

You have to think anyway, so why not think big?
–Donald J. Trump

Joe Biden (2021 –)

- He uses the word "malarkey" more than most people, including in the 2010 vice presidential debate. During the 2020 campaign he had a #nomalarkey bus tour through Iowa.
- He carries a holy rosary everywhere that he goes; the one he carries now was his son Beau's (Beau died in 2015 from brain cancer).
- He stuttered growing up until a friend in law school helped him to shake it by reading poetry out loud.
- He has never drunk alcohol because his family has a history of alcoholism.
- He was elected to the Senate at the age of 29, and turned 30, the minimum age to be eligible, by the time he was sworn in.

INGREDIENTS

2 ounces Powers Irish whiskey
½ ounce Nocello
½ ounce Luxardo cherry liqueur
Scrappy's Orleans bitters
    (3 dashes)
Garnish: Luxardo maraschino
    cherry

PREPARATION

Combine all ingredients in a cocktail shaker with ice and shake well. Strain into a martini glass. Garnish with cherry.

*All our differences hardly measure up to
the values we all hold in common.*
–Joe Biden

Epilogue

The 45 days leading up to the Election Day contest between Donald J. Trump and Joseph R. Biden were not easy ones for us, or millions of others around the country. These 45 days were shaped by endless drama, general tumult, a cascade of falsehoods, politicization of facemasks, scientific naysaying, close to 250,000 deaths attributable to COVID-19, a SCOTUS controversy, racially-charged protests and riots following the deaths of Black civilians at the hands of police, millions more impoverished and hundreds of thousands more jobs lost, conspiracy theories...and so much additional tragedy and suffering outside the U.S. as well.

Luckily for us, this project provided a much-needed distraction...and the cocktails helped too!

There is, however, much room for hope. In spite of the pain and division—or, one could argue, because of it—we saw record-shattering levels of voter turnout in every state, territory, and the District of Columbia. Well over 150 million Americans saw through the exaggerations and misinformation about potential or perceived fraud that were propagated in social media, political commentary and electioneering, and exercised the right to vote.

The citizens of these United States of America demanded to be heard. We did so in defiance of the virus. We did so in early voting, absentee voting, mail-in voting and, finally, at polling sites on Election Day. (Jeremy had the honor—and anxiety—of being the poll Judge at a location here in Dallas. Andy had to put up with his obsessive sense of duty and detail.) We're proud to see our great state of Texas and our county (Dallas) shatter all previous voting numbers. As a nation, we should be proud of what can be seen as a renaissance in voter participation in the governing of our great republic. There is, as always, hope for the future.

info@cocktailhourmeets.com

Fin

About the Authors

Andy and Jeremy currently live in Dallas, Texas, and have been together since 1997. When not working, or quarantined at home, they enjoy traveling, eating, cooking, entertaining new and old friends, and discovering and sampling new wines, tequilas, and whisk(e)ys. Feel free to reach out to either of them with questions or comments.

info@cocktailhourmeets.com

Made in the USA
Middletown, DE
14 November 2020